HANDBOOKS OF EUROPEAN NATIONAL DANCES

EDITED BY

VIOLET ALFORD

DANCES OF THE NETHERLANDS

Plate 1
Volendam

DANCES OF THE NETHERLANDS

E. VAN DER VEN-TEN BENSEL

NOVERRE PRESS

ILLUSTRATED BY
ROWLAND A. BEARD
ASSISTANT EDITOR
YVONNE MOYSE

First published in 1953
This edition published in 2021 by
The Noverre Press
Southwold House
Isington Road
Binsted
Hampshire
GU34 4PH

ISBN 978-1-914311-1-23-9

© 2021 The Noverre Press

CONTENTS

INTRODUCTION	Page 7
The Cramignon, a Chain Dance	8
Dances from the Achterhoek	9
An Important Square Dance	12
Feasts and Customs	13
Dances of Ritual Origin	14
Historical Dances	15
National Dance Revival	16
Music	17
Costumes	18
WHEN DANCING MAY BE SEEN	21
THE DANCES	22
Poise of Body and Arm Holds	23
Basic Steps	24
Horlepijp	25
Driekusman	27
De Skotse Trije	32
De Zevensprong	36
BIBLIOGRAPHY	39

Illustrations in Colour, pages 2, 19, 30, 31
Map of the Netherlands, page 6

INTRODUCTION

O NE of the most cheerful and characteristic expressions of folk life everywhere is national dance, but this delightful trait cannot be found in every corner of our country. In Holland proper, that is the provinces of North and South Holland, we are faced with conditions somewhat different from those in most countries—the predominance in Dutch life of town over country. The growth of towns in a small country carrying a large population naturally spreads town ways, and this we find almost from the moment when Holland emerged as a cultural entity. The human geography of our land worked strongly in the same direction also, for when the new lands were reclaimed from the sea in the seventeenth century, the new inhabitants were not country folk bred in the love of old traditions, but a puritanical, Calvinistic population who brought with them a fear, not to say a hatred, of dancing and any sort of merrymaking. In the new lands therefore no such cheerful doings took root.

Our western and northern regions form a marked contrast to those of the south and east. Here live country folk, long settled on the old lands, who never accepted the reformed religion, who have from time immemorial occupied themselves with agriculture, celebrating the numerous communal, seasonal festivities always attached to that mode of life.

In spite of a few enclaves in the north, we can draw a rough line with western and northern Holland on one side of it, southern and eastern Holland on the other. One side of this line is poor in traditional rites and dances; the other, the southern and eastern side, offers a rich variety of traditions, in which a number of simple dances play a part. In the extreme south of Limburg, in the village of Eijsden, and in the small town of Ootmarsum more to the east, two distinct types of old ritual Chain dances are still alive. A fortnight after Whitsuntide, the villagers of Eijsden celebrate their feast—a Church procession on the Sunday, and a fair during the following days. On the Monday and Tuesday the jollifications reach their culminating point in a dance in which everyone must join—the Cramignon.

THE CRAMIGNON, A CHAIN DANCE

This is one form of the Europe-wide Chain dance which stretches from the Mediterranean to the Baltic, and further. The dancers, joining hands, form a long chain the leader of which is the captain of the bachelors' or young men's club. This leader often carries a bunch of flowers in his free hand as his insignia of office, and he takes his followers in and out of the houses and inns of the village. The brass band goes in front of the long, sinuous line, and it is easy for anyone to join the chain. The step is nothing but a continued lively, skipping step, subsiding into a walk or shuffle when the dancers get out of breath. The Cramignon is also danced on festive occasions in several other villages of Limburg, but nowhere else has it remained so closely allied to folk ritual as at Eijsden.

Its slow counterpart is the Easter Processional dance of Ootmarsum, called Vlöggelen. Here the chain, of sometimes over a thousand dancers, is led by eight men, the Poaskerls (Easter-men), and in this immense coiling line the people all move together with measured walking step, singing a beautiful old Easter carol, *Christus is opgestanden* ('Christ has risen'). The leader places one hand behind him into which the next Poaskerl lays his, the whole chain joining up in the same fashion, and so that they shall not forget the words of the carol the dancers pin a sheet with the printed text on their backs for the man behind to read as he processes.

DANCES FROM THE ACHTERHOEK

The wider region round Ootmarsum, with the adjoining Achterhoek of Gelderland, is a centre where old traditions have happily lived until the present time. Nowhere in the Netherlands have the regional dances remained more popular at fairs, weddings and on national feast days than here. Local fiddlers, accordion players and brass bands all can, and often will, play the traditional tunes. When, in between modern dances, they strike up one of the old favourites it is a delight to see young and old join in the dance. In several of the villages and small country towns in this district the inhabitants have formed groups for the regular practice of their regional dances and for the preservation of their traditional costumes, which, alas, in everyday life have almost disappeared. One such club, from the village of Gorssel, showed their dances at the International Folk Dance Festival in London, 1935. They were directed in loud, authoritative tones by their village dancing master, a fine and impressive figure, wielding as the insignia of his important office a stout stick gaily decorated with ribbons and flowers.

The Achterhoek dances comprise dances both for groups and for pairs. Although nowadays all have a recreational character, in one a ritual source is still traceable. This is apparent in both words and movements in *Riepe, Riepe Garste* (Ripe, Ripe Rye), which must certainly have been a Harvest dance. Practically all these Achterhoek dances except the Squares have words sung by the dancers. I give a short list of such dances with a translation of their names:

Onze Broeder Lazarus (Our Brother Lazarus)
Lot is Dood (Lot is Dead)
Waar is Jan met de Meid? (Where is John and his Girl?)
De Hoaksebarger (The Hoaksebarger dance)
De Smid (The Smith)
De Driekusman, also known as Het Hendriekske
Onze Fikshond het Vleu (Our Dog has Fleas)

An assortment of names stretching from the Scriptures to low animal life! Most of these have slightly different variants, often with other names, in other parts of the Netherlands. For instance, 'Where is John and his Girl' is known as De Slaapmuts (The Nightcap) in the province of North Holland, and goes to the words and tune of *Flip die Vleugelt* on the island of Terschelling. All three are variants of one dance, which under the name of Duitsche Polka (German Polka) was once known all over Holland. Therefore enquiry into names is important in this country. The Hoaksebarger has been localised, and from its name and its accompanying words has been assigned to the village of Haaksbergen. It is, however, not only found in other parts of the Netherlands—for instance in Limburg as De Vottendans—but all over Northern Germany too. In Denmark it is popular, and occurs in Sweden as Snurrebock,* where it is called a *komisk allmogedans*, a comic country dance. All variations in all these countries show the same sequence—a slow stately promenade, followed by a quick Gallop or a Polka. This is interesting, for it recalls a very usual medieval dance-sequence—a slow introduction followed by a quick stepping movement. In the Achterhoek version the comic quality is rather crudely emphasised. In the introductory part of De Hoaksebarger the partners walk solemnly hand-in-hand, singing in their local dialect:

Ik ben met mien mèke noa Hoaksebarge west, bo joa!
(I have been with my girl to Haaksbergen, oh yes!)

* See *Dances of Sweden* in this series.

To which last words partners bow, and turning abruptly bow in the other direction, exclaiming:

Bo, nei! (Oh no!)

and resume their dignified walk.

In contrast with the above dances, which are all with Polka step, 'Our Dog' is a variation of the once fashionable Mazurka. The most popular of these Gelderland dances, De Driekusman, or Het Hendriekske, has variants in countries as far apart as Sweden, Bohemia, Poland and Czechoslovakia. Het Piasterke, a variant of Driekusman, in the island of Terschelling, shows men and women vis-à-vis in two lines, like those of an English Longways Country dance, while the usual forms show miming movements together with a couple dance. The Squares still in vogue with the rural population of the Achterhoek may be identified as degenerate Quadrilles and Lancers, except one named Horlepijp (Hornpipe). The step here is more intricate, or shall I say less simple, than in any other Dutch folk dance, and may perhaps have originated from a sailor's step, though found far from the sea. The Vleegerd, another Achterhoek Square, is simple to a degree, but never fails to make its effect, especially when shown to a town audience, who seem to consider the figures eminently in accordance with their ideas of rusticity. The climax, repeated over and over again each time the men change partners, consists of 'throwing' them—and it is pretty literally throwing—into the arms of the opposite man. The girls shriek, the audience roars with appreciative laughter. The rustic impression is heightened by the wooden shoes of the dancers stressing the rhythm. These wooden shoes are the most characteristic feature of the Gelderland costume, for the women's black nineteenth-century peasant dresses with their small white caps and the men's old-fashioned Sunday best offer nothing very striking, though the plain black and white makes a good contrast.

The remaining Achterhoek Squares are countrified Lancers or Quadrilles. They are:

Peerdesprong (The Horse's Jump)
Keppelsche Quadrille (Keppel Quadrille)
Geldersche Boerendans (Gelderland Peasant Dance)

I need not go into details of figures which sufficiently indicate their once fashionable origin, but will only say that one of these variants, called by the country people Anna van Duinen, at first sight a girl's name, seems to have a more amusing meaning. If we remember the dance direction *en avant deux* frequently occurring in the Quadrilles and Lancers, the corruption of this French phrase becomes apparent. Similar corrupted Quadrilles have been retained in other parts of Holland, in the province of North Brabant, for instance.

AN IMPORTANT SQUARE DANCE

Best-known all over Holland, belonging to no particular district, is the so-called 'Frisian Square', Skotse Trije. When therefore the Frisians wish to show off something as their own possession, they dress in the wonderful festive costume of their grandparents, which, to tell the truth, is not a peasant costume but the sumptuous attire of the rich middle classes and aristocracy. Skotse Trije often alternates its figures with verses from It Skoenmakerke (The Shoemaker's Dance), which is a singing game rather than a dance. *Skotse*, it has been suggested, means Scotch, and that the dance was introduced by the Scottish brigades quartered in Friesland between 1572 and 1783—more than two centuries. But it is more likely to be connected with the Swedish *skotar*. *Trije* may be 'three', but again it is more likely to belong to the *Treiros*, *Treieres* form of words occurring in medieval songs whose root is *tro*, *troi* or *trei*, meaning 'to turn'—like Portuguese *virar*, from which the name of the Vira is derived.

In West Friesland Skotse Trije is to be found also, but under the name of Donder in het Hooi (Thunder in the Hay). This is apparently a case of mistaken folk etymology, for the Hey (the reel or figure of eight) on each side of the dance set is an often-repeated figure.

FEASTS AND CUSTOMS

Until the First World War the greatest variety of dances—connected till then with Midsummer and Midwinter ritual—were found on the island of Terschelling, that island of ours which rises right out of the North Sea. The two great annual festivals of the island population, which has in its isolation preserved many a folk rite, are a Midwinter and a Midsummer festival, the latter celebrated on a Sunday about a fortnight after the feast of St. John the Baptist, which is Midsummer Day. On this day—the most important in seasonal reckoning since pre-Christian times and long before St. John's name became connected with it—villagers ride in decorated carts to the common where the festival is to be celebrated with much eating and drinking, singing and dancing. Before leaving the village they take a last drink, the 'St. John's cup', and the gay carts drive three times round the Church, then on to the village common where dancing alternates with songs to the accompaniment of violin and accordion. Until about sixty or seventy years ago an image of St. John was taken in the procession of carts, and dances were performed round it on a special piece of common land called St. John's Corner. After the 1914–18 War the Midsummer festival, which was already unique in Holland, gradually lost its lustre. When in 1923 the Dutch folklorist D. J. van der Ven took a detailed film of the dances, it was practically the last time the feast was celebrated in its glory. Then the old islanders danced in their sailors' dress, and their partners in their typical black island gowns with black bonnets. Nowhere in the Netherlands have I found such high dance quality as in the performance of these Terschelling fishing people, although the dances themselves are simple.

In the Rielen, the agility of the men shows up well as they continually and quickly swing one leg behind the other in a *pas battu*. Another of their dances is a Round in which a man and a woman alternately goes into the ring to choose a partner. It is traditional for every Terschelling festival to wind up with the Wilhelmus dance and the Afklappertje. Singing a queer version of the Dutch National Anthem, corrupt in both tune and words, couples walk arm-in-arm round a circle. When the musician strikes up a version of the well-known 'Malbrouck' the dancers obediently draw up in two lines, partners facing each other, and with much clapping and stamping they proceed with a progressive Longways Country dance. When each couple has been at the top they finish with the walking procession once more.

DANCES OF RITUAL ORIGIN

Of all our dances, that which has best preserved its ritual character is the Seven Jumps. It used to be performed round the image of St. John, and when it was filmed in 1923 only men took part as tradition prescribed. While singing

> *Heb je niet gehoord van de sie, sa, seven,*
> *Heb je niet gehoord van de zevensprong?*

(Have you not heard of the Seven Jumps?)

the men walk round in a circle holding hands; to the words *Da's een* (That's one) they stamp with the right foot. On the repeat they stamp with right and left. On every repeat one movement is added. Finally they touch the ground with their foreheads, and to show their agility will turn head over heels. This strange dance has its counterparts in several European countries, notably the Basque countries both Spanish and French; no doubt we can connect all these with the ritual jumping to make the corn grow tall.

The most popular of our Rounds, performed by grown-ups as well as children, as a kissing dance at wedding parties and other boisterous occasions, is De Patertje (The Friar), with its parallels De Govert in North Holland, and Japie sta stil (John stand still) on the island of Schiermonnikoog. Japie walks into the middle of the ring playing all sorts of ridiculous tricks, singing a solo meanwhile, followed by a refrain sung by all. The words of both these Rounds show that once upon a time they were May dances, in which John and the Friar chose a girl to be May Queen. But to-day only in Valkenburg, a small town in Limburg, is the May Queen chosen—on April 30, immediately after the planting of the Maypole. The Terschelling image of St. John most probably took the place of the ancient Maypole, always so disapproved by the clergy; so we may perhaps add the Seven Jumps to a Maypole tradition, also the dance round a huge Whitsuntide garland performed in a popular quarter of the old town of Deventer. Another dance reminiscent of ancient men's ritual was the North Brabant Besom dance, now obsolete.

HISTORICAL DANCES

In town archives all over the Netherlands there are plenty of entries bearing witness to the various Morris and Sword dances which constantly appeared until the general penetration of Calvinism. The earliest date mentioning a Sword dance in this country is found in the archives of Dordrecht, 1392, only three years later than the first known record for Europe, which is that of a Bruges Sword dance in 1389; in fact just about the period these most ancient of dances were becoming stylised into town shows in the hands of the Guilds. A very valuable testimony as to the popularity of Sword and Stick dances is furnished by the countless prohibitions against them. In spite of this, according to the records of towns such as Nijmegen, Kampen and

Deventer, the Sword dancers were at the same time sumptuously regaled by the very magistrates who condemned them. In the southern part of Zeeland the Wapenreiers, as the Sword dancers were called there, held frequent competitions, so the records tell us. In the town of Middelburg the archives mention a Moressendans performed by the Guild of Shoemakers in 1553, and in 1568 the Morris of Tholen came to add lustre to the Church procession of Breda. It is a pity that in these, as in a great number of other records, no details at all are given as to figures and steps in either Sword dance or Morris.

More instructive than city archives is the picture by Pieter Breughel the Younger, in which we see all sorts of interesting things going on at a fair, about the end of the sixteenth century. Besides people enjoying a Longways Country dance, drinking, feasting and fighting, there is a Sword dance going on in the centre of the village square. The eleven dancers are all dressed alike and have just reached the figure known as Single Under. We can study them at leisure, fixed for ever at their village feast by the miraculous and meticulous brush of their painter.

A similar lack of information is met with as regards the Egg dance. It too has been pictured in an oil painting by Pieter Aertsen about 1557, and again in 1618 we see it in an engraving by Joh. de Brij. It was a ritual dance of agility, and in Switzerland is performed about Eastertime, while Dutch colonists who went to the isle of Amager near Copenhagen have kept it alive until just recently, though lost at home.

NATIONAL DANCE REVIVAL

This survey would not be complete without a few words about the folk-dance revival which has taken place in the Netherlands during the last thirty years. In accordance with the present-day tendency for group activities in the renewal of social life, inspiration has naturally been sought in the past, when music and dance still furnished a satisfying expression of communal life. Since the nineteenth-century Dutch dances in their simple and somewhat contaminated forms did not offer a very rich nor varied material, youth leaders introduced dances from neighbouring peoples. Thus German and Scandinavian dances became favourites, but since 1927 literally thousands of my compatriots have applied themselves to learning and enjoying English Morris, Sword and Country dances. The strong appeal which English national dances have had in the Netherlands can be explained by their superior aesthetic quality, and by their intrinsic value as group dances.

But we have never considered the practice of foreign dances in Holland as an end in itself. Any renaissance which has ever successfully taken place has looked upon the past as a starting-point only. Old forms and old ideas have always given rise to new creations from which springs renewed life. Otherwise a revival would be barren indeed. So we look upon the present moment as a transitional stage in the life of Dutch national dances, and look forward to the creation of typical Dutch forms to prove that the old material has borne its fruit for the present generation. With our cultural and social revival, possibilities will surely develop so that by and by new, but typically Dutch, national dances may well come into being.

MUSIC

The brass band plays a large part in the life of Dutch villages. The great chain of the Cramignon is accompanied by the village band, but the Vlöggelen, that immense religious Chain used for the Easter Procession, is accompanied only by the singing of the ancient Easter carol. Local accordionists used to accompany dancers all over the country, but even this later instrument is now dying out, and its place taken by small bands consisting of violin, clarinet, double-bass and drum seen at weddings, fairs and other festivities.

But the greater number of Dutch dances demand their own dance-songs, and the words of these are repeated over and over again by the dancers, who never seem to weary of them, and who are frequently aided, when short of breath, by the bystanders. The words are generally lost under the noise of the accordion or the band, but the dancers seem to know them, and still to enjoy the traditional use of them and their tunes.

COSTUMES

It is unfortunate that our rural populations with the most striking costumes have no dances of their own. The Island of Marken, one of the best-preserved enclaves for costumes in North-West Europe, possesses no dance, and the islanders never do dance, either folk dances or any others. The next best region for costumes, Zeeland, again has no dances of its own, and when the islanders feel moved to dance they indulge in the Seven Jumps, which is not their particular property but belongs to the whole country. The same thing holds good for the Volendam villagers, also dancing the Seven Jumps at their October fair. These are the people who wear what is called Dutch costume by foreigners, and which appears on the stage of every country in Europe as such, in drawings boorish and romantic, and at performances of every dancing school to dress a comic character number. We know it all too well—the fishermen with their baggy trousers, their partners with enormously wide checked skirts and white caps. What we do not see are the red coral necklaces and the seven or eight petticoats worn beneath the skirt, though the young generation now prefers a pleated black skirt which gives a slim and even elegant outline. In any case this is not the costume for any Dutch dance but the Seven Jumps.

Plate 2
Friesland: Burgher's costume

For the Driekusman plain costumes are worn, the main feature of which are the wooden shoes which stamp out the rhythm when required. The women wear stiffly made nineteenth-century black dresses, or a long brown skirt with a coloured jacket, flowered or striped; dress or skirt of good thick material, jacket of cotton or silk; aprons light in colour or white; red coral necklaces; white cotton caps with a small flounce at the back, and often gold rings hanging from the cap in front. The men put on their old-fashioned Sunday clothes with black silk caps, or the clothes of a former generation, or a long blue cotton peasant blouse.

For Skotse Trije, Friesland people wear the beautiful dress of the old landed aristocracy and rich burghers; silk dresses in lovely colours; fichus of valuable white lace, as are the aprons. On their heads they wear closely fitted caps of real gold, covered with white lace and decorated with real diamond pins. The men wear black frock-coats and dignified tall hats. Men and women alike dance in low black shoes with silver buckles.

SOME OCCASIONS WHEN DANCING MAY BE SEEN

Easter Sunday and Monday — Vlöggelen Processional at Ootmarsum.

A Fortnight after Whitsuntide (Sunday, Monday and Tuesday) — The Cramignon at Eijsden, Limburg Fair.

During May and June — The Cramignon at Limburg villages other than Eijsden, at village feasts. Dates must be ascertained. At weddings, frequently celebrated in May. The Achterhoek dances at farms in Overijsel and Gelderland.

A Fortnight after St. John's Day (Midsummer) — The Terschelling dances used to be performed but are now irregular, and it must be ascertained whether this festival is to be held or not.

All through the summer — Local and regional folklore and historical societies' gatherings with dances and costumes.

Third week in October — Volendam fisherfolks' fair. Their favourite dance is the Seven Jumps. Here is worn the best-known Dutch costume.

THE DANCES

TECHNICAL EDITOR, MURIEL WEBSTER
ASSISTED BY KATHLEEN P. TUCK

ABBREVIATIONS
USED IN DESCRIPTION OF STEPS AND DANCES

r—right ⎱ referring to   R—right ⎱ describing turns or
l—left ⎰ hand, foot etc.   L—left ⎰ ground pattern
C—clockwise   C-C—counter-clockwise

For descriptions of foot positions and explanations of any ballet terms the following books are suggested for reference:

A Primer of Classical Ballet (Cecchetti method). Cyril Beaumont.

First Steps (R.A.D.). Ruth French and Felix Demery.

The Ballet Lover's Pocket Book. Kay Ambrose.

REFERENCE BOOKS FOR DESCRIPTION OF FIGURES:

The Scottish Country Dance Society's Publications. Many volumes, from Thornhill, Cairnmuir Road, Edinburgh 12.

The English Folk Dance and Song Society's Publications. Cecil Sharp House, 2 Regent's Park Road, London, N.W.1.

The Country Dance Book I–VI. Cecil J. Sharp. Novello & Co., London.

POISE OF BODY AND ARM HOLDS

Many of the square dances are countrified versions of the Lancers or Quadrilles and will therefore be danced with a certain amount of dignity. This is especially true of the Skotse Trije because the sumptuous costumes call for a dignified and upright carriage. In the freer couple dances where rhythm is strongly stressed by wooden shoes, movements are more rolling and boisterous.

As many of the dances are Chain or Square formation, arm gestures are limited. In the Cramignon chain dance, the leader carries a bunch of flowers in his free hand. In the Easter processional chain dance Vlöggelen, each dancer places one hand behind him into which the hand of the next dancer is laid. In some of the couple dances partners walk side by side hand-in-hand or arm-in-arm. If the dance ends with a Polka the men hold their partners with both hands round their waists, and the girls put their hands on the men's shoulders.

The group and couple dances of Gelderland are often accompanied by singing, and in this case the dancers suggest the actions by mime and gesture.

BASIC STEPS

Skipping Step (as in Cramignon).

Danced in a lively manner, subsiding into a walk or shuffle as the dancers get out of breath.

Walking Step:

(a) As in Vlöggelen—in a processional manner to fit the carol which is sung.

(b) As in any couple dance.

Polka:

(a) A heavy step without a hop—one Polka step to each bar (as in Driekusman and De Skotse Trije).

(b) A gay step (as in Horlepijp).

HORLEPIJP (Hornpipe)

Region	Achterhoek. Plates 3 and 4.
Character	Recreational and to show agility.
Formation	Four to eight couples in a loose circle round dancing space. They hold inside hands or link arms.

Dance

MUSIC
Bars
A

1 Long step forward on r foot. [*Beat 1*]   1

Close l foot behind r, bringing weight on to l. [*and*]

Step forward on r. [*Beat 2*]

Step to L on l foot. [*and*]

Close r behind l, taking weight on to it.   2
[*Beat 1*]

Swing l leg behind r. [*and*]

Jump and land on both feet, l crossed behind r. [*Beat 2*]

Do this four times in all.   3–8

B

2 8 Polka steps turning and moving C-C   9–16
round the room, grasping as described under
Arm Holds.

Repeat the whole dance as often as desired.

Note.—Variations of figures may be used in this dance, but the Hornpipe step is always danced to A music and Polka step to B music.

HORLEPIJP

From the Achterhoek
Arranged by Arnold Foster

Suggested variations
The following figures may be used when eight couples perform the dance:

A MUSIC. Rings of four couples; rings of two couples; partners facing each other; women's ring in centre, men's ring outside them.

B MUSIC. Couples make arches; partners pass back to back; big ring moving C-C and C; partners turn each other.

DRIEKUSMAN or HENDRIEKSKE

		MUSIC
Region	Achterhoek. Plates 3 and 4.	
Character	Recreational, all entering into the fun of the mime and the well-marked rhythm of the Polka.	
Formation	As many couples as will, forming a double ring, partners facing each other, men with back to centre. All have hands on hips.	

Dance

	MUSIC
	Bars
	A
1 Swing upper part of body to R and then L.	1
Clap three times.	2
Repeat movements of Bar 1.	3
Stamp three times, r l r.	4

Threaten partner with r forefinger three times.	5
Repeat with l forefinger.	6
All make a whole turn to R and face partner again.	7–8
Repeat movements of Bars 1–8.	1–8
	B
2 Men hold partners with both hands round their waists and women put their hands on men's shoulders. In this position they dance round C-C with 16 rather heavy Polka steps without a hop.	9–16 repeated
Repeat the whole dance several times.	

DRIEKUSMAN

From the Achterhoek
Arranged by Arnold Foster

A Well marked

Met de händ-jes, klap, klap, klap, Met de vöt - jes,

stap, stap, stap, Har ik di'j, wat zol, ik di'j!

Plate 3

Plate 4

DE SKOTSE TRIJE (*The Skotse Turn*)

Region — Known all over Holland as the regional folk dance of the Frisians. Plate 2.

Character — With dignity and a good carriage of the body.

Formation — A Square dance for eight couples. In each line of four dancers the two women stand between two men (○ = woman, □ = man).

```
       □ ○ ○ □
      □         □
      ○         ○
      ○         ○
      □         □
       □ ○ ○ □
         FRONT
```

Dance

| | MUSIC Bars |

Throughout the dance a Polka step without a hop is used; one step to each two bars of music.

A

1 Top and bottom lines, holding hands, move towards each other with two Polka steps.   1–4

SKOTSE TRIJE

From Friesland
Arranged by Arnold Foster

C

Top and bottom lines, still holding hands, move backward to their places with two Polka steps.	5–8
Side lines repeat movements of top and bottom lines.	1–8

B

2 All dancers, holding hands in a ring, dance round C with 4 Polka steps. — 9–16

Still holding hands, all dance back to places moving C-C with 4 Polka steps. — 9–16

C

3a Women from each line join r hands and move towards centre of set with 2 Polka steps. At the same time the men on each corner join r hands and move to centre of set. — 17–20

All, still holding r hands, move backward to places with 2 Polka steps. — 21–24

Partners, holding r hands, repeat the movement of Bars 17–24. — 25–32

3b Straight hey for four on each side of the set; partners start facing each other and pass r shoulders. This will take eight Polka steps, and each line should finish with the two men in the middle, and the two women on the corners of the square. Each will pass r shoulders round the two end loops and l shoulders in the middle, as in a hey for three or four in an English Country Dance, but move on one extra place. — 17–32

The whole dance is repeated until the dancers finish in their original places.

DE ZEVENSPRONG (*The Seven Jumps*)

Region	Volendam. Plate 1.
Character	With mock solemnity. Dancers sing the words of the song as they dance.
Formation	Circle for any number of couples holding hands in a ring.

Dance	MUSIC
All travel C, facing the centre of the circle.	*Bars*

FIRST TIME:

Chorus. 16 walking steps or 8 Polka steps without a hop.	1–8
One jump. On the words 'Da's een' all stamp r foot.	9

SECOND TIME:

Chorus. Repeat movements of Bars 1–8.	1–8
Two jumps. All stamp first r foot then l foot.	9–10

After each repetition of the walking or Polka steps C, the dancers add one new movement, so that the LAST TIME the sequence is as follows:

Chorus	
16 walking steps or 8 Polka steps as before.	1–8

DE ZEVENSPRONG

From Volendam
Arranged by Arnold Foster

Have you never heard of the / si sa seven,

Have you never heard of the / seven jumps?

Do you really think that / I can't dance it?

I / dance it like a /nobleman. That's one, that's two, etc.

Seven jumps
  (1) Da's een—stamp r foot.   9
  (2) Da's twee—stamp with l foot.   10
  (3) Da's drie—kneel on r knee.   11
  (4) Da's vier—kneel on both knees.   12
  (5) Da's vijf—place r elbow on ground.   13
  (6) Da's zes—place both elbows on ground.   14
  (7) Da's zeven—lie flat on ground.   15

NOTE

The traditional costumes of the Netherlands are quite other than what is popularly supposed to be 'Dutch'. The costume thus mistakenly named is that of Volendam only and it is neither 'fancy' nor comic. Respect, then, these historic costumes, as their wearers respect them, and do not dress town dancers of Skotse Trije in an attempt at a comic country dress.

The Editor

BIBLIOGRAPHY

(The volumes marked with asterisks contain only notations and tunes.)

* BROM-STRUICK, W.—*Reidansen*, Vols. I and II. 1927 (reprinted 1947), W. L. Brusse, Rotterdam. (Dutch country dances.)
* VAN CREVEL, M.—*Reidansen*, Vol. III. 1934, W. L. Brusse, Rotterdam. (English country dances.)
ELOUT, C. K.—*In kleuren en kleeren*. 1931, Algemeen Handelsblad, Amsterdam. (Descriptions of costumes, with coloured illustrations.)
KNOP, GERRIT.—*Schylgeralân*. 1946, Burgersdijk & Niermans, Leiden. (The island of Terschelling.)
KUNST, JAAP.—*Terschellinger Volksleven*. 1915, H. H. Fongers, Uithuizen. (Terschelling folk life; illustrated.)
VAN DER LEEUW, PROF. DR. G.—*In den hemel is eenen dans*. 1930, Amsterdam. ('There is a dance in Heaven.')
MOLKEMBOER, T. H.—*Onze nationale Kleederdrachten*. 1915. (National costume; illustrated.)
* REINHOLDA, ZUSTER.—*Lentelust. Meiekinderen. Vroolijk Volkje*. Three volumes of series 'Volksdansen voor de jeugd'. (Folk dances for young people.) 1933, Tegelen.
RÖNTGEN, JULIUS, and D. J. VAN DER VEN.—*Nederlandsche Boerendansen*. 1923, Vereeniging voor Noord-Nederlandsche Muziekgeschiedenis, Amsterdam. (Dutch peasant dances.)
* SANSON-CATZ, A., and A. DE KOE.—*Oude Nederlandsche Volksdansen*. 2 vols. 1927, 1929, Staal & Co., Rotterdam. (Old Dutch folk dances.)
* TIGGERS, LINE.—*Pinksterblom. Bonte Rei*. 2 vols. 1929, Arbeidersjeugd-Centrale, Amsterdam. (The May Queen.)
VAN DER VEN, D. J.—*Neerlands Volksleven*. 1920, Zalt-Bommel. (Dutch folk life; illustrated.)
VAN DER VEN, D. J.—*Onze Nederlandsche Jeugd in nationale dracht*. 1927, Haarlem. (Dutch children in national dress; illustrated.)
VAN DER VEN, D. J.—*Onze Nederlandsche Volksdrachten*. Rutgers, Naarden (in the press). (Dutch folk costumes; illustrated.)
VAN DER VEN–TEN BENSEL, DR. ELISE.—*De Volksdans in Nederland*. 1942, Rutgers, Naarden. (Folk dance in the Netherlands, with illustrations and dance-notations.)

van der Ven–ten Bensel, Dr. Elise.—'30 Contradansen.' 1931, *De Spieghel*, Amsterdam. (30 country dances transcribed from the English.)

van der Ven–ten Bensel, Dr. Elise.—*De Volksdans Herleeft*. 1933, G. W. den Boer, Middelburg. (The revival of folk dance; illustrated.)

van der Ven–ten Bensel, Dr. Elise.—'15 gemakkelijke contradansen.' 1934, *De Spieghel*, Amsterdam. (15 easy country dances, transcribed from the English.)

van der Ven–ten Bensel, Dr. Elise.—'10 Mannendansen.' 1934, *De Spieghel*, Amsterdam. (10 men's dances, transcribed from the English.)

van der Ven–ten Bensel, Dr. Elise.—'Volkszang en Volksdans' in *Volk van Nederland*. 1942, Elsevier, Amsterdam. (Folk song and folk dance; illustrated.)

van der Ven–ten Bensel, Dr. Elise.—'Dutch Folk Dances.' 1931, *The Journal of the English Folk Dance Society*.

van der Ven–ten Bensel, Dr. Elise.—*De Volksdansmare*, 1932–1939. (Magazine with illustrations.)

Veurman, B.—*Westfriesche Volksliederen en Dansen*. 1943, Martinus Nijhof, The Hague. (West Frisian folk songs and dances, with dance-notations.)

de Witt Huberts, Fr.—*Zwaarddansen*. 1931, Santpoort. (Sword dances; illustrated.)

www.ingramcontent.com/pod-product-compliance
Lightning Source LLC
Chambersburg PA
CBHW061744290426
43661CB00127B/972